Learn and Play with

Tails

Jesus and Me Every Day

Bible
Heroes and Helpers

"See, God will help me"
Psalm 54:4

Karyn Henley

BROADMAN
& HOLMAN
PUBLISHERS

US Edition published in 2000
by Broadman & Holman Publishers
Nashville, Tennessee

Originally published by CWR, Waverley Abbey House, Waverley Lane, Farnham, Surrey GU9 8EP, England

Tails: Bible Heroes and Helpers

© 1999 Karyn Henley. All rights reserved. Exclusively administered by Child Sensitive Communication, LLC
Text and characterizations by Karyn Henley

Concept development, editorial, design and production by CWR
Models created by: Debbie Casto
Photographed by: Roger Walker
Illustrations: Sheila Hardy of Advocate
Printed in England by Linneys Colour Print
ISBN 0-8054-2287-0
Published 2000 by Broadman & Holman Publishers

Identified Scripture quotations are from the Holy Bible, New International Version, copyright ©1973, 1978, 1984 by International Bible Society.

All other Scripture quotations in this publication are from the Holy Bible: International Children's Bible copyright © 1983, 1988, 1991 by Word Publishing.

Welcome to Tails! Tails is written especially for young children, because of their unique needs and interests. Young children are strongly affected by story. So the Tails series presents not only Bible stories, but application stories and activities using animal characters. Young children will grow to love and identify with these animal friends. In return, the Tails characters will help introduce young children to the Bible, to God, and to godly values.

Each book in the Tails series focuses on a simple theme and memory verse that are meaningful to the young child. Using one page a day, the parent, teacher, or caregiver can take the child through an entire month of theme-related scriptures, devotional thoughts, and fun activities. We suggest that as you participate in personal or family daily devotions, you include your child by guiding him or her through a page of the Tails book.

Of course, you may wish to use the Tails books as a supplement to Bible study materials. You may also use them as fun, Bible-based activity books for occasions when the child travels, or is sick in bed, or otherwise needs the companionship of his or her Tails friends.

We are confident that your young child will enjoy Tails. It is our privilege and pleasure to provide this enjoyable way for your child to grow in knowing and loving God.

By God's grace, to His glory,

Karyn Henley

Meet the Tails Friends

Welcome to Tails Town. You'll see that each of us has a different kind of tail. We have other kinds of tales, too: the stories we tell. Our favorite stories are about God. He has given each of us different tails to wear and different tales to tell. That reminds us that even though we are all different, we can work together and love each other. And that pleases God.

Mimi

Hi, friends! My name is Mimi. Let me paint my name for you. What color? Hmmmm. All the colors of the rainbow! If I painted your name, what color would you want me to use? I like all kinds of art. I like to paint and draw and make all kinds of crafts. If you ever want to find me, look for me in my art corner!

Owlfred

Helloo–oo–oo! My name is Owlfred. I'm an explorer. I like to find out how things work or why things sound or feel or look the way they do. So I like to do experiments. I try things to find out what will happen. I'll help you to find things out too. Or I might give you a puzzle or ask a question to find out what YOU think.

Chester

What's up, new friends? My name's Chester. Do you like FUN? Then come with me! If there's an adventure around, I'm ready to jump right in. I love all kinds of games. If you'd like, I'll make up some games just for you. So come on along and have some FUN.

Tennyson

Ahoy there! Tennyson is my name, and I'm a poet.
  I write poems and rhymes.
  And songs sometimes.
  See there? I knew it.
  Somehow I just do it.
If you sit quietly with me, we'll see sights and hear sounds and learn about our feelings. Then I'll write a poem for you. And you can write a poem for me.

Mrs H

Hello! I'm Mrs. H. Are you ready for a snack? Whenever you're hungry, come into my kitchen. You'll always find something good to eat there. I'll show you how to make some of the yummiest treats you ever tasted. At least, Twigs thinks they're yummy.

Twigs

Mmmm! Yes! Are the treats ready to eat now? My name is Twigs, and I need to pack a snack for the day, because I'm going to explore with Owlfred. Then I want to watch Mimi paint. And I might play a game with Chester. Then I'll rest by the pond with Tennyson, and we'll write a song about my busy day.

Yes, it's a busy day in Tails Town! Turn the page and join us!

A Place to Stay

WHO-OO-OO can say the verse?

"See, God will help me."

Psalm 54:4

Elisha went to many different towns telling people about God. In one town, a lady and her husband built an upstairs room on their house. It was a room just for Elisha. It had a bed, a table, a chair and a lamp in it. So Elisha had his own room when he came to their town. The lady and her husband helped Elisha by giving him a place to stay. (2 Kings 4:8-10)

The Place Where I Live

Elisha had a bed, table, chair, and lamp in his room. What do you have in your room? Draw it in the house shape below.

God helps you. God has given you a place to stay. Thank You, God!

A Prayer

Dear God,
Thank You for giving me a place to stay. Amen.

Tennyson's Rhyme Time

Tennyson has written a song for Twigs to sing. See if you can sing it and do the actions.

2

Here is the roof-top, here are the walls

Look out the win-dow, tip-toe down the halls (tiptoe)

Here is the ta-ble Where I sit to eat, and

Here is the bed where I go to sleep.

Thank you, God. z-z-z-z (can you snore?)

Where does Tennyson sleep?

The Real God

Elijah loved God. He built an altar* of stones. He put meat on it. That was part of the way he worshipped God.

Other men did not love God. They thought there was a different god named Baal. They built an altar to worship Baal. They prayed to Baal and asked him to send fire to burn the meat on their altar. They prayed and prayed. But no fire came.

Elijah prayed to God and asked God to send fire for his altar. God sent fire right away! God showed that He was real. God helped Elijah by answering his prayer. (1 Kings 18:16–39)

*This is what an altar looks like. It's like a big campfire on top of a tall pile of big rocks. You can color this altar with a crayon, or press your thumb onto a washable ink pad or onto a bit of paint. Then press your thumb onto each stone.

There are sticks of wood on this altar. Color fire coming down from the sky onto the altar.

A Prayer

Dear God,
Thank You for hearing me when I pray. Thank You for answering prayers. Amen.

God helped Elijah by answering Elijah's prayer. Elijah helped God by telling other people about God. He shared God's words with other people. You can share God's words with other people. You can share other things too. In each picture below, something is missing. Draw the thing that's missing in the spaces below.

If someone needs food, you can share food.

If someone needs a coat, you can share a coat.

If someone needs a toy to play with, you can share a toy.

If someone needs to be cheered up, you can be a friend. You can share a smile.

If someone needs a drink of water, you can share a drink.

If someone needs a place to sit, you can share your seat.

I lost it!

Some men were building a place to live. They used axes to cut down trees. They used the trees to make boards. They used the boards to build a house.

While one man was cutting down a tree, the top of his axe fell off. It fell into the water. "Oh no!" he said. "That was not my axe! I had borrowed it!"

Elisha was there. The man showed him where the axe top fell. Then Elisha cut a stick. He threw it onto the water. The axe top floated up to the surface of the water, and the man pulled it out.

Elisha helped. Who helped Elisha make the axe top float? (2 Kings 6:1–7)

Get a bowl. Fill it with water. Find some small things around your house, like a rock, a piece of paper, a bottle cap, a button, a plastic or wooden spoon, a cork, and other things. Place these things one by one on the water.

Find out if they float or sink.

Owlfred's Experiment

- Things that are lighter than water will float.

- Things that are heavier than water will sink.

- But even heavy things that are shaped like a bowl will float.

A Prayer

**Dear God,
Thank You for caring about the things we lose. Thank You for helping us. Amen.**

Elisha helped the man find his axe top. You can help mom or dad or a friend look for things they have misplaced or lost. In the picture below, Twigs and Mrs. H are looking for some things they have lost. Can you help?

I will, I won't

Once there were two boys. Their dad told the first boy to go and work in the garden. But the first boy said, "No." After a while, the first boy changed his mind. He did go and work in the garden.

The dad told the second boy to go and work in the garden. The second boy said, "All right. I'll go." But then he changed his mind. He did not go to work in the garden. Which boy helped his dad? (Matthew 21:28–31)

This is the first boy. He helped. Draw his happy helper face.

This is the second boy. He did not help. Draw his sad face.

The dad wanted his boys to work in the garden where he grew grapes. You can make a grape picture by pushing your thumb into blue or purple washable ink or paint. Then press your thumb under the grape leaf and stem, like the picture of the grapes on the left.

To make purple paint, try mixing red with blue. You need only a little bit of paint to make these grapes. If you want, you can make them with crayons instead of paint.

Sometimes we need special tools to use when we help. In the kitchen, we might need spoons and mixing bowls and measuring cups.

Chester's Challenge

Look at the pictures below. Draw a circle around the pictures of tools that you might use to help in the garden.

A Prayer

**Dear God,
Give me a helping heart. When someone asks me to help, help me to say, "Yes. I will!" Amen.**

Looking for a donkey

Jesus needed to ride on a small donkey when He went to the big city. Two of Jesus' friends helped. They went to look for a donkey that He could ride. They found the donkey and brought it back to Jesus. They even put their coats on the donkey's back so Jesus would have a soft place to sit. They were helpers. (Mark 11:1–11)

Sing along and do the actions with Chester!

Tennyson's Rhyme Time

Who will help pick up toys?

Who will help pick up toys?

Who will help?   I will! I will!

Who will help and not make noise?

Who will help?   I will! I will!

Who will help wash the dish?

Who will help?   I will! I will!

Who will help feed the fish?

Who will help?   I will! I will!

Who will help?

Who will help sweep the stairs?

Who will help?   I will! I will!

I will! I will!

Who will help say the prayers?

Who will help?   I will! I will!

A Prayer

Dear God,
Show me how to help. Make me into a happy helper.
Amen.

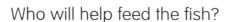

Jesus' friends helped Him by finding the donkey. And Jesus helped His friends by telling them exactly where to look. You can get a friend to help you make a paper donkey. Then your friend can hide it and help you find it.

Mimi's Art Corner

Make a donkey from an envelope. Ask a grownup for help. Cut the envelope like the picture shows below. Use the folded cut off part to make a head. Cut it as shown. Slip it over the back of the donkey and tape it in place.

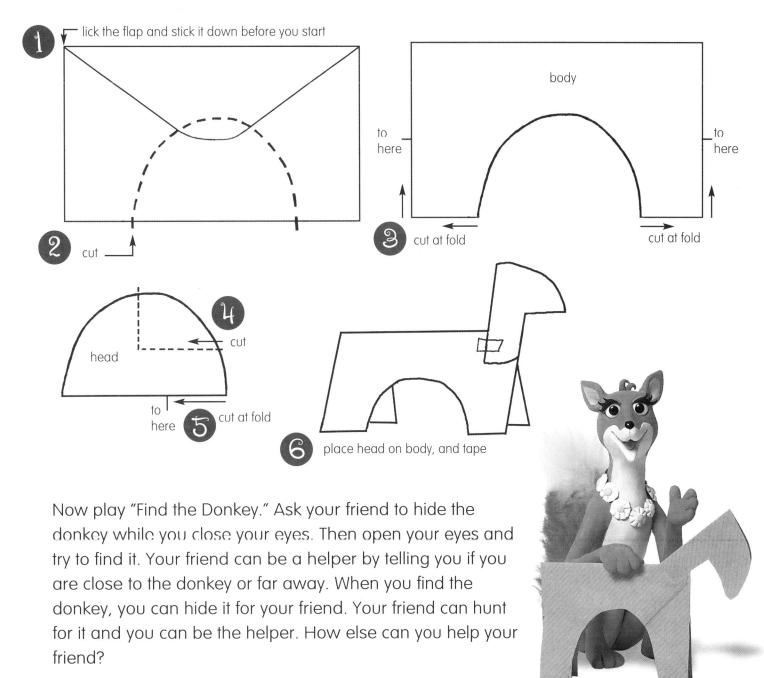

1 lick the flap and stick it down before you start

body

to here

to here

2 cut

3 cut at fold   cut at fold

4 cut

head

to here

5 cut at fold

6 place head on body, and tape

Now play "Find the Donkey." Ask your friend to hide the donkey while you close your eyes. Then open your eyes and try to find it. Your friend can be a helper by telling you if you are close to the donkey or far away. When you find the donkey, you can hide it for your friend. Your friend can hunt for it and you can be the helper. How else can you help your friend?

Bringing home the food

Ruth and Naomi lived together. Naomi was older. She could not do hard work. But somebody had to work to get food for them to eat. So Ruth worked. She worked hard all day. At night, she brought food home, and they ate. Ruth helped Naomi. Ruth was a helper. (Ruth 2)

Twigs goes shopping with his mom. They buy food to take home. Here is Twigs with his shopping cart. Fill his cart by drawing food in it. How do you help when you go to buy food?

Please can we have these? I like these best!

WHOO-OO-OO remembers the verse?

"See, God will help me."

Psalm 54:4

A Prayer

Dear God,
Thank You for helping my family get food to eat. Help me to be a helper at home too. Amen.

Ruth helped Naomi in other ways too. And Naomi helped Ruth. When Ruth got married and had a baby, Naomi helped take care of the baby. She held the baby in her lap.

Taking care of a family at home is hard work. How do you help at your house? Do you help clean? Do you help cook?

Ruth's job was gathering grain from the field. The grain she gathered was barley. Wheat is also grain. Oats are grain too. Here is something you can help make at home with oats.

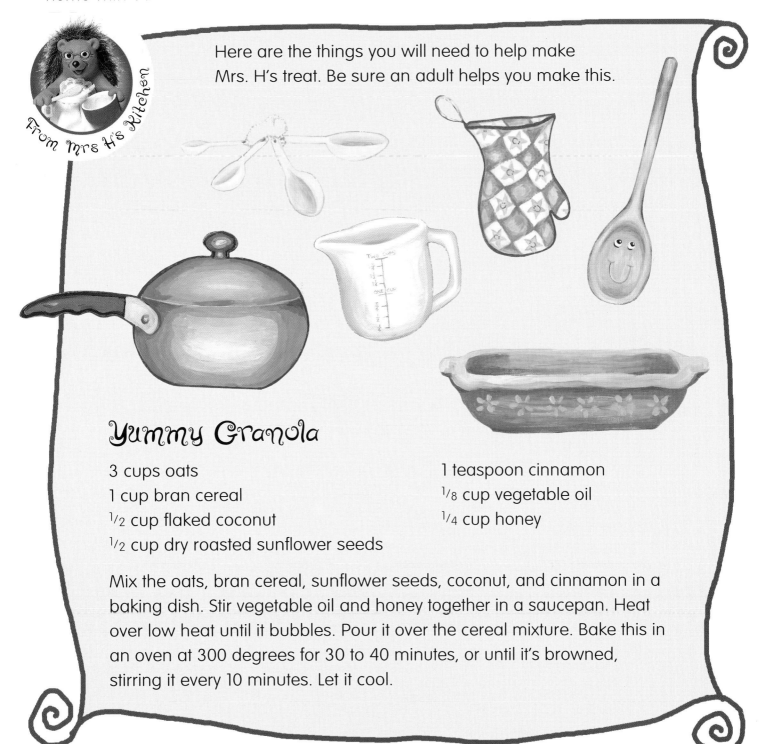

From Mrs H's Kitchen

Here are the things you will need to help make Mrs. H's treat. Be sure an adult helps you make this.

Yummy Granola

3 cups oats
1 cup bran cereal
$1/2$ cup flaked coconut
$1/2$ cup dry roasted sunflower seeds

1 teaspoon cinnamon
$1/8$ cup vegetable oil
$1/4$ cup honey

Mix the oats, bran cereal, sunflower seeds, coconut, and cinnamon in a baking dish. Stir vegetable oil and honey together in a saucepan. Heat over low heat until it bubbles. Pour it over the cereal mixture. Bake this in an oven at 300 degrees for 30 to 40 minutes, or until it's browned, stirring it every 10 minutes. Let it cool.

Watching the baby

Miriam had a baby brother. She helped her mom take care of the baby. But there was a mean king who wanted to kill the baby boys of Miriam's people. So Miriam's mother tried to hide the baby. She made a special basket. She put the baby in the basket and let it float on the water in the river. The basket rocked back and forth on the water, and Miriam helped by watching the basket. She ran to get her mom when the baby needed help. (Exodus 2:1 – 10)

Here are some helper's baskets holding the tools the helper needs. Look at the tools in each basket. See if you can tell the job of the helper who uses those tools.

Chester's Challenge

Miriam had another brother named Aaron. Miriam was the big sister, Aaron was the big brother. Do you know who the baby in the basket was? His name was Moses. Moses was the baby brother.

Do you have a baby brother or sister in your family? Do you have friends who have a baby in their family? How can you help when you are with a baby?

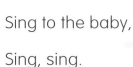

Rock the baby,

Rock, rock.

Sing to the baby,

Sing, sing.

Pat the baby,

Pat, pat.

Quiet for the baby,

Shhh! Shhh!

Point to the things in the picture below that you might need to help take care of a baby.

A Prayer

Dear God,
Help me to be a gentle helper when I am with a baby.
Amen.

Thirsty camels

Rebekah's family needed some water. They did not have a sink. So Rebekah carried a big jar to the well outside. The well went deep into the ground. There was water in the well. Rebekah dipped her jar into the well and filled the jar with water.

A man walked up to Rebekah. The man had camels with him. "Can you give me some water?" asked the man.

"Yes," said Rebekah. "I'll give your camels some water too." Rebekah was a helper. She gave the man a drink of water. She gave his camels a drink too. (Genesis 24:1–27)

Do you have a pet? Draw a picture of your pet in Mimi's picture frame. If you don't have a pet, draw a picture of a pet that belongs to a friend or grandparent, or even a pet that you would like to have.

Mimi's Art Corner

A Prayer

Dear God,
Thank You for pets. Help me to be a helper with my pets
and with the pets that belong to my friends. Amen.

Animals get hungry and thirsty. Rebekah gave the camels some water. What are some things you can do to help with your pet or a friend's pet?

Did you ever go to a pet shop? Here is a picture of a pet shop. But all the pets got mixed up. They need to be put back where they belong. Can you help by showing where each pet belongs?

Joseph, the helper

Joseph loved God. And Joseph was a hard worker. Joseph worked for a man named Potiphar. Joseph took care of Potiphar's house. God helped Joseph do a good job of taking care of everything. When Joseph was working, Potiphar did not have to worry about anything. Joseph was a very good helper. (Genesis 39:1–5)

Crumple some old newspaper into small balls, middle sized balls and big balls. Try throwing them into a waste paper bin. How far away can you stand and still get the paper in?
Is it easier to throw the small balls, the middle sized balls, or the big balls?

Chester's Challenge

Taking out the trash is one way you can help around your house.

A Prayer

Dear God,
Thank You for giving me a place to live. Help me to be a helper around my house. Amen.

Potiphar trusted Joseph to work hard and do a good job. When people work hard and do a good job, we say they are **dependable**. Joseph was **dependable**. When Potiphar told Joseph to clean the room, Joseph cleaned the room. Joseph obeyed. Who tells you to clean your room? Do you obey? Are you a dependable helper?

Twigs needs to clean his room. Look at Twigs' room to see what he needs to do to clean up.

Now look at your room. Is there anything you need to do to make your room neat and clean?

Water to drink

Moses was a leader for God's people. God told Moses what to do and where to go. Moses told God's people what to do and where to go. Moses was God's helper.

One day the people could not find any water to drink. God told Moses, "I will show you a big rock. Hit the rock with your stick. Water will come out."

So Moses went to the big rock that God showed him. He hit the rock with his stick. Water came out for all the people to drink. Moses was a helper. (Exodus 17:1–7)

From Mrs H's Kitchen

Does a friend sometimes come to play with you? How can you help when your friend gets thirsty? What is your favorite drink? Here's a drink that Twigs likes to share with his friends.

Banana-Pineapple Punch

1 cup orange juice
1/2 cup pineapple juice
1/4 teaspoon lemon juice
1 crushed banana
1/2 cup lemon-lime soda or carbonated water

Mix orange juice, lemon juice, pineapple juice and banana. Then gently stir in the lemon-lime soda or carbonated water.

A Prayer

**Dear God,
Show me how to help my friends. Help me to be a happy helper. Amen.**

Moses helped get the water that God's people needed. Everybody needs water to drink. Where does water come from?

God made water and put it in rivers and seas all over the world. Some of the water becomes water vapor* that we can't even see. It floats up high into the sky. Then it mixes with dust and turns into clouds. The clouds get heavier and heavier with water vapor until the water vapor becomes heavy drops of water that fall back down to the earth as rain. The rainwater flows into the earth and back to the rivers and seas again. Thank You, God, for Your plan for water.

Draw more clouds in the sky.

Color the clouds a dark color. Make lots of rain.

Color the rivers and the seas.

WHOO-OO-OO remembers the verse?
"See, God will help me."
Psalm 54:4

*Have you ever seen steam go up from a pan or a cup of hot water? That steam is water vapor.

A helper under a palm tree

Where does your dad or mom go to work? Some dads and moms work in office buildings. Some work at stores or shops. Deborah was a lady who worked under a palm tree. When people had trouble with each other, they went to Deborah. They told her about their trouble. Deborah helped them by telling them who was right and who was wrong. She helped them decide what to do. Do you have a helper like that at your house? (Judges 4:4, 5)

This is a palm tree.

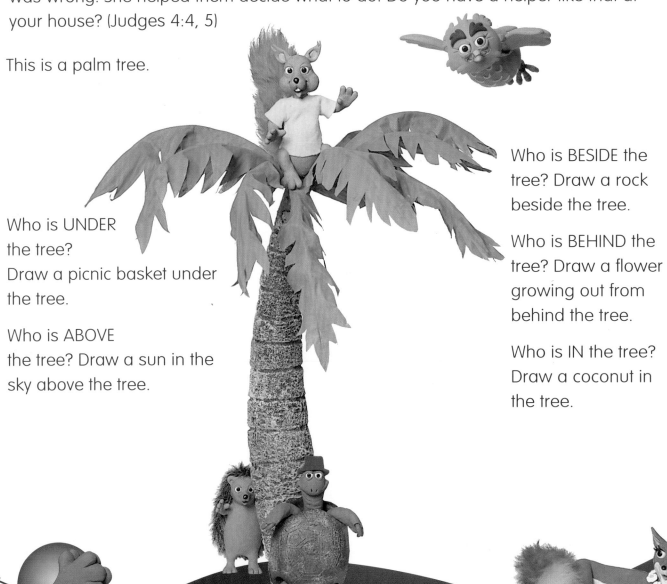

Who is UNDER the tree? Draw a picnic basket under the tree.

Who is ABOVE the tree? Draw a sun in the sky above the tree.

Who is BESIDE the tree? Draw a rock beside the tree.

Who is BEHIND the tree? Draw a flower growing out from behind the tree.

Who is IN the tree? Draw a coconut in the tree.

A Prayer

Dear God,
Thank You for people who help me to know what's right and what's wrong. Help me to choose what's right. Amen.

Deborah tried to help people settle their arguments. Then the people could still be friends. How can you help people settle their arguments? When you have an argument with a friend, who can you ask to help you?

Mimi and Chester have had an argument. They both want to paint a picture, but there's only one paintbrush. How can they settle their argument? Do you have any ideas about what they could do?

There's only one brush, and I want to use it.

No, no! Let me. I want to paint!

Did you think of some of these ideas?

- Take turns. Toss a coin to see who goes first. One paints a picture. Then the other paints a picture.
- Use a timer. Mimi paints for 5 minutes, then Chester paints for 5 minutes.
- Get something else to paint with, like a sponge or an old toothbrush or a feather. Paint at the same time.
- Make a game of add-on. Mimi paints one thing in the picture. Then Chester adds something else in the picture. Then Mimi adds something else, and so on.

But now it's your turn! Draw a picture on the art paper for Mimi and Chester.

 # God helps David

You can help read this story. When there is a picture, you can say the word for that picture.

Once there was a named David who took care of  .  's dad

said, " , I want you to take this and to your .

They are near the  where they will help the to fight the enemy."

So took the and to his  . When he got there a

marched out from the enemy . The said, "Send someone out

to fight me." 's were 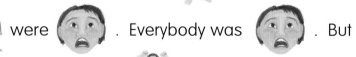 . Everybody was . But

was not . said, "I will fight the . God will help me."

 went to the and picked up  . put one

in his . twirled his around and around. Then threw

the out towards the . The hit the  in the , and the

fell down dead. God had helped win!   (1 Samuel 17)

God helps us when we love and obey him. David wrote, "... in God I trust; I will not be afraid" (Psalm 56:4, NIV). David trusted God. David knew God would help him. You can trust God too. You can know that God will help you.

Here is Tennyson's song about David and the giant.

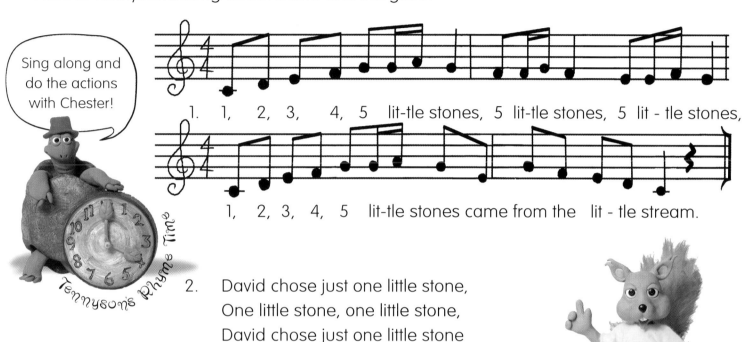

Sing along and do the actions with Chester!

1. 1, 2, 3, 4, 5 lit-tle stones, 5 lit-tle stones, 5 lit - tle stones, 1, 2, 3, 4, 5 lit-tle stones came from the lit - tle stream.

2. David chose just one little stone,
One little stone, one little stone,
David chose just one little stone
To put into his sling.

3. The little stone went 'round and around,
'Round and around, 'round and around.
The little stone went 'round and around
and shot into the air.

4. It hit the giant ker-thump in the head,
Thump in the head, thump in the head.
It hit the giant ker-thump in the head,
And then the giant fell down . . .

CRASH!   (spoken)

A Prayer

**Dear God,
Thank You for helping me. I trust in You like David did. I will not be afraid. Amen.**

A Queen asks for help

Queen Esther needed to talk to the king. But the rule was that you could go to see the king only if he asked you to come. If you did not wait to be asked, you were in big trouble! You could even be killed!

But Queen Esther was one of God's people. And some mean people were trying to kill God's people. So Queen Esther needed to ask the king for help.

First the queen prayed to God for help so she would be brave enough to go and see the king. The queen's friends prayed for her too. Then Queen Esther went to see the king. The king was happy to see the queen. He was not angry. So Queen Esther asked the king for help, and he helped God's people. (Esther 4, 5, 7, 8)

Sometimes we need to ask other people to help us. It's always best to ask kindly and to say "please".

Tennyson wants to borrow a book of stories from Owlfred. How should he ask? When Owlfred gives him the book, what should Tennyson say?

Twigs needs help to cross the street. How should he ask? When someone helps him, what should Twigs say?

Chester wants Mimi to help him paint a picture to hang on his wall. How should he ask? When Mimi helps him, what should Chester say?

God made our bodies so we can help each other. How can your  help someone? How can your  help someone?

How can your s help someone? How can your

help someone?

Take your sock and shoe off one foot. Stand up with your bare foot on the blank space above on this page. With a pencil or crayon, trace around your foot. You can ask someone for help if you need to.

How can your feet help someone? How does God help you? When we ask God for help, how should we ask? When God helps us, what should we say?

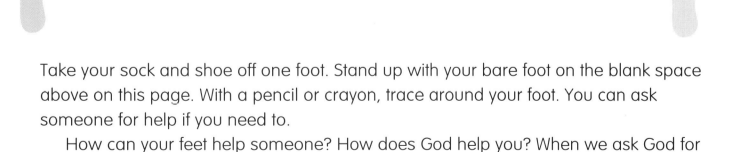

A Prayer

Dear God,
Thank You for helping me. I love You. Amen.

A helper with a donkey

There was once a man who was hurt very badly. He was lying by the side of the road. Another man came walking by. He saw the hurt man. But he did not stop to help. A second man came walking by. But he did not stop to help. Then a man came by with a donkey. This man stopped. He helped the hurt man. He let the hurt man ride on his own donkey to a place where somebody could take care of him. (Luke 10:25–37)

Here is the helper with a donkey. Help him find the way to the place where the hurt man is. Then find the path to the place where someone will take care of him.

A Prayer

Dear God,
Thank You for helping me when I'm hurt. Help me to help others when they are hurt. Amen.

You can read many stories in the Bible that tell how God helped sick people get well. You can help sick people feel better by doing things for them.

1. Pray for God to make them well.

2. Take them something to eat or drink.

3. Read a Bible story to them or sing a song for them.

4. Help them find a soft place to lie down and rest. Bring them pillows and blankets.

5. Make a GET WELL card and send it to them.

Mimi's Art Corner

To make a GET WELL card, take a piece of plain paper. Fold it in half like a card or book.

Draw a picture on front of the card. You can draw one on the inside, too, if you want. If you need help, ask an older person to write GET WELL on the front. Sign your name on the inside. Give it to someone who is sick, or put it in an envelope and send it to a sick person. Remember to pray for the sick person too.

GET WELL SOON

A little is a lot

Sometimes we help other people by giving them money. Some people need money to buy food or clothes or a place to stay. Some people need money to go to other countries and teach people about Jesus. We can help by giving some of our money.

Once Jesus was watching people give money at the temple church. Rich people gave lots of money. But one lady gave only two coins. Jesus said she gave the most, because those two coins were all the money she had. (Mark 12:41–44)

Lots of Coins

Put two coins under this page behind the blank space below. Rub over the space with a crayon or pencil to show the coin shapes underneath. Then move the two coins to another place below and rub over them again. Keep moving them around and rubbing over them to make it look as if there are lots and lots of coins. When you are finished, count them. How many coins are there?

WHOO-OO-OO remembers the verse?

"See, God will help me."

Psalm 54:4

Sometimes we have only a little bit of money to give to help someone. But if we give a little and someone else gives a little, all together, there is enough to help.

The Tails friends know that Bitsy Bear needs some warm winter clothes. Nobody has enough money to buy the clothes. But together, they can buy something. Look at how much money they have and find what they can buy together.

Tennyson has 4. Owlfred has 4. Together what can they buy for Bitsy?

Mimi has 3. Chester has 3. Together what can they buy for Bitsy?

Mrs. H has 3. Twigs has 2. Together what can they buy for Bitsy?

Draw the warm winter clothes on Bitsy Bear.

A Prayer

Dear God,
Thank You for helping me. Help me to help others.
Amen.

A beautifully illustrated story book is available to accompany this devotional activity book. **Twigs has an Adventure** features all the Tails friends, as they rush to the aid of Twigs, who has found that his adventures have taken him just a little too high up a tree! As Owlfred flies in to rescue Twigs, all the animals delight in understanding firsthand the key verse from this devotional "See, God will help me." (Available in hardback.)

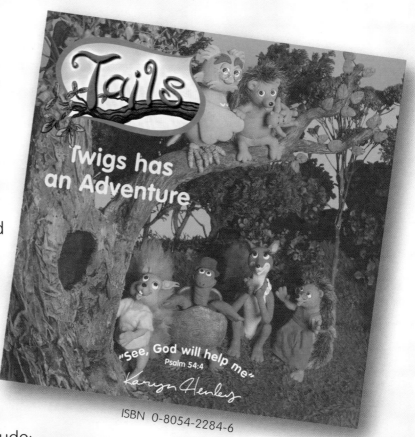

ISBN 0-8054-2284-6

Other devotional activity books and accompanying story titles include:

Who is God? ISBN 0-8054-2288-9

King for a Day ISBN 0-8054-2285-4

Sunlight and Starry Night
ISBN 0-8054-2286-2

A Noise in the Woods
ISBN 0-8054-2197-1